Christina Georgina Rossetti, The Poetry

Poetry is a fascinating use of language. With almost a million words at its command it is not surprising that these Isles have produced some of the most beautiful, moving and descriptive verse through the centuries. In this series we look at individual poets who have shaped and influenced their craft and cement their place in our heritage.

Christina Georgina Rossetti was born in London in 1830 one of four children who were all to become artists and writers. Educated at home, her life was filled with the Italian influences of her Father and the wide ranging interests of her mother. She began to write at age 12 just at the time her Fathers health broke and the family descended to near poverty. She was first published aged 18 and over the following decade her writing was to flourish and in 1860 her most famous work Goblin Market was released and her reputation was set. A sufferer from Graves disease from the 1870's she also developed breast cancer which subsequently recurred and was to cause her death in 1894. She is buried in Highgate Cemetery.

Many of the poems are also available as an audiobook from our sister company Portable Poetry. Many samples are at our youtube channel http://www.youtube.com/user/PortablePoetry?feature-mhee The full volume can be purchased from iTunes, Amazon and other digital stores. Among our readers are David Shaw-Parker, Ghizela Rowe and Richard Mitchley.

Index Of Poems

A PAUSE OF THOUGHT
A STUDY (A Soul)
BITTER FOR SWEET
BY THE SEA
FERRY ME ACROSS THE WATER
GOODBYE IN FEAR GOODBYE IN SORROW
IF ALL WERE RAIN AND NEVER SUN
IF STARS DROPPED OUT OF HEAVEN
IS THE MOON TIRED? SHE LOOKS SO PALE
LONG BARREN
MIX A PANCAKE
ONE SEA SIDE GRAVE
REQUIEM
SAPPHO
SONNETS ARE FULL OF LOVE
WIFE TO HUSBAND
GOBLIN MARKET
AN OCTOBER GARDEN
CHRISTMAS EVE
GOOD FRIDAY
A YEARS WINDFALLS
HOW MANY SECONDS IN A MINUTE
WHO HAS SEEN THE WIND
AN EMERALD IS AS GREEN AS GREEN
IN THE BLEAK MIDWINTER
WINTER – MY SECRET

JANUARY COLD DESOLATE
AFTER THIS JUDGEMENT
AFTER DEATH
DEAD BEFORE DEATH
LIFE AND DEATH
REMEMBER
A BETTER RESURRECTION
DE PROFUNDIS
DREAM LAND
PASSING AWAY, SAITH THE WORLD
THE CONVENT THRESHOLD
THE THREAD OF LIFE
BIRD RAPTURES
TWILIGHT CALM
COBWEBS

A PAUSE OF THOUGHT
I looked for that which is not, nor can be,
And hope deferred made my heart sick in truth:
But years must pass before a hope of youth
Is resigned utterly.

I watched and waited with a steadfast will:
And though the object seemed to flee away
That I so longed for, ever day by day
I watched and waited still.

Sometimes I said: This thing shall be no more;
My expectation wearies and shall cease;
I will resign it now and be at peace:
Yet never gave it o'er.

Sometimes I said: It is an empty name
I long for; to a name why should I give
The peace of all the days I have to live?—
Yet gave it all the same.

Alas, thou foolish one! alike unfit
For healthy joy and salutary pain:
Thou knowest the chase useless, and again
Turnest to follow it.

A STUDY (A Soul)
She stands as pale as Parian statues stand;
Like Cleopatra when she turned at bay,
And felt her strength above the Roman sway,
And felt the aspic writhing in her hand.
Her face is steadfast toward the shadowy land,

For dim beyond it looms the light of day;

Her feet are steadfast; all the arduous way
That foot-track hath not wavered on the sand.
She stands there like a beacon thro' the night,
A pale clear beacon where the storm-drift is;
She stands alone, a wonder deathly white;
She stands there patient, nerved with inner might,
Indomitable in her feebleness,
Her face and will athirst against the light.

BITTER FOR SWEET
Summer is gone with all its roses,
Its sun and perfumes and sweet flowers,
Its warm air and refreshing showers:
And even Autumn closes.

Yea, Autumn's chilly self is going,
And winter comes which is yet colder;
Each day the hoar-frost waxes bolder,
And the last buds cease blowing.

BY THE SEA
Why does the sea moan evermore?
Shut out from heaven it makes its moan,
It frets against the boundary shore;
All earth's full rivers cannot fill
The sea, that drinking thirsteth still.

Sheer miracles of loveliness
Lie hid in its unlooked-on bed:
Anemones, salt, passionless,
Blow flower-like; just enough alive
To blow and multiply and thrive.

Shells quaint with curve, or spot, or spike,
Encrusted live things argus-eyed,
All fair alike, yet all unlike,
Are born without a pang, and die
Without a pang, and so pass by.

FERRY ME ACROSS THE WATER
'Ferry me across the water,
Do, boatman, do.'
'If you've a penny in your purse
I'll ferry you.'
'I have a penny in my purse,
And my eyes are blue;
So ferry me across the water,
Do, boatman, do.'

'Step into my ferry-boat,
Be they black or blue,
And for the penny in your purse
I'll ferry you.'

GOODBYE IN FEAR GOODBYE IN SORROW
'Goodbye in fear, goodbye in sorrow,
Goodbye, and all in vain,
Never to meet again, my dear'
'Never to part again.'
'Goodbye today, goodbye tomorrow,
Goodbye till earth shall wane,
Never to meet again, my dear'
'Never to part again.'

IF ALL WERE RAIN AND NEVER SUN
If all were rain and never sun,
No bow could span the hill;
If all were sun and never rain,
There'd be no rainbow still.

IF STARS DROPPED OUT OF HEAVEN
If stars dropped out of heaven,
And if flowers took their place,
The sky would still look very fair,
And fair earth's face.
Winged angels might fly down to us
To pluck the stars,
Be we could only long for flowers
Beyond the cloudy bars.

LONG BARREN
Thou who didst hang upon a barren tree,
My God, for me;
Though I till now be barren, now at length
Lord, give me strength
To bring forth fruit to Thee.

Thou who didst bear for me the crown of thorn,
Spitting and scorn;
Though I till now have put forth thorns, yet now
Strengthen me Thou
That better fruit be borne.
Thou Rose of Sharon, Cedar of broad roots,
Vine of sweet fruits,
Thou Lily of the vale with fadeless leaf,
Of thousands Chief,
Feed Thou my feeble shoots.

MIX A PANCAKE
Mix a pancake,
Stir a pancake,
Pop it in the pan;
Fry the pancake,
Toss the pancake,
Catch it if you can.

ONE SEA SIDE GRAVE
Unmindful of the roses,
Unmindful of the thorn,
A reaper tired reposes
Among his gathered corn:
So might I, till the morn!

Cold as the cold Decembers,
Past as the days that set,
While only one remembers
And all the rest forget, -
But one remembers yet.

REQUIEM
When I am dead, my dearest,
Sing no sad songs for me;
Plant thou no roses at my head,
Nor shady cypress tree:
Be the green grass above me
With showers and dewdrops wet;
And if thou wilt, remember,
And if thou wilt, forget.

I shall not see the shadows,
I shall not feel the rain;
I shall not hear the nightingale
Sing on, as if in pain:
And dreaming through the twilight
That doth not rise nor set,
Haply I may remember,
And haply may forget.

SAPPHO
I sigh at day-dawn, and I sigh
When the dull day is passing by.
I sigh at evening, and again
I sigh when night brings sleep to men.
Oh! it were far better to die
Than thus forever mourn and sigh,
And in death's dreamless sleep to be
Unconscious that none weep for me;
Eased from my weight of heaviness,

Forgetful of forgetfulness,
Resting from care and pain and sorrow
Thro' the long night that knows no morrow;
Living unloved, to die unknown,
Unwept, untended, and alone.

SONNETS ARE FULL OF LOVE
Sonnets are full of love, and this my tome
Has many sonnets: so here now shall be
One sonnet more, a love sonnet, from me
To her whose heart is my heart's quiet home,

To my first Love, my Mother, on whose knee
I learnt love-lore that is not troublesome;
Whose service is my special dignity,
And she my loadstare while I go and come
And so because you love me, and because
I love you, Mother, I have woven a wreath
Of rhymes wherewith to crown your honoured name:
In you not fourscore years can dim the flame
Of love, whose blessed glow transcends the laws
Of time and change and mortal life and death.

WIFE TO HUSBAND
Pardon the faults in me,
For the love of years ago:
Good-bye.
I must drift across the sea,
I must sink into the snow,
I must die.

You can bask in this sun,
You can drink wine, and eat:
Good-bye.
I must gird myself and run,
Though with unready feet:
I must die.

Blank sea to sail upon,
Cold bed to sleep in:
Good-bye.
While you clasp, I must be gone
For all your weeping:
I must die.

A kiss for one friend,
And a word for two,
Good-bye:
A lock that you must send,
A kindness you must do:
I must die.

Not a word for you,
Not a lock or kiss,
Good-bye.
We, one, must part in two;
Verily death is this:
I must die.

Goblin Market
Morning and evening
Maids heard the goblins cry:
"Come buy our orchard fruits,
Come buy, come buy:
Apples and quinces,
Lemons and oranges,
Plump unpecked cherries
Melons and raspberries,
Bloom-down-cheeked peaches,
Swart-headed mulberries,
Wild free-born cranberries,
Crab-apples, dewberries,
Pine-apples, blackberries,
Apricots, strawberries
All ripe together
In summer weather
Morns that pass by,
Fair eves that fly;
Come buy, come buy;
Our grapes fresh from the vine,
Pomegranates full and fine,
Dates and sharp bullaces,
Rare pears and greengages,
Damsons and bilberries,
Taste them and try:
Currants and gooseberries,
Bright-fire-like barberries,
Figs to fill your mouth,
Citrons from the South,
Sweet to tongue and sound to eye,
Come buy, come buy."

Evening by evening
Among the brookside rushes,
Laura bowed her head to hear,
Lizzie veiled her blushes:
Crouching close together
In the cooling weather,
With clasping arms and cautioning lips,
With tingling cheeks and finger-tips.
"Lie close," Laura said,
Pricking up her golden head:

We must not look at goblin men,
We must not buy their fruits:
Who knows upon what soil they fed
Their hungry thirsty roots?"
"Come buy," call the goblins
Hobbling down the glen.
"O! cried Lizzie, Laura, Laura,
You should not peep at goblin men."
Lizzie covered up her eyes
Covered close lest they should look;
Laura reared her glossy head,
And whispered like the restless brook:
"Look, Lizzie, look, Lizzie,
Down the glen tramp little men.
One hauls a basket,
One bears a plate,
One lugs a golden dish
Of many pounds' weight.
How fair the vine must grow
Whose grapes are so luscious;
How warm the wind must blow
Through those fruit bushes."
"No," said Lizzie, "no, no, no;
Their offers should not charm us,
Their evil gifts would harm us."
She thrust a dimpled finger
In each ear, shut eyes and ran:
Curious Laura chose to linger
Wondering at each merchant man.
One had a cat's face,
One whisked a tail,
One tramped at a rat's pace,
One crawled like a snail,
One like a wombat prowled obtuse and furry,
One like a ratel tumbled hurry-scurry.
Lizzie heard a voice like voice of doves
Cooing all together:
They sounded kind and full of loves
In the pleasant weather.

Laura stretched her gleaming neck
Like a rush-imbedded swan,
Like a lily from the beck,
Like a moonlit poplar branch,
Like a vessel at the launch
When its last restraint is gone.

Backwards up the mossy glen
Turned and trooped the goblin men,
With their shrill repeated cry,
"Come buy, come buy."

When they reached where Laura was
They stood stock still upon the moss,
Leering at each other,
Brother with queer brother;
Signalling each other,
Brother with sly brother.
One set his basket down,
One reared his plate;
One began to weave a crown
Of tendrils, leaves, and rough nuts brown
(Men sell not such in any town);
One heaved the golden weight
Of dish and fruit to offer her:
"Come buy, come buy," was still their cry.
Laura stared but did not stir,
Longed but had no money:
The whisk-tailed merchant bade her taste
In tones as smooth as honey,
The cat-faced purr'd,
The rat-paced spoke a word
Of welcome, and the snail-paced even was heard;
One parrot-voiced and jolly
Cried "Pretty Goblin" still for "Pretty Polly";
One whistled like a bird.

But sweet-tooth Laura spoke in haste:
"Good folk, I have no coin;
To take were to purloin:
I have no copper in my purse,
I have no silver either,
And all my gold is on the furze
That shakes in windy weather
Above the rusty heather."
"You have much gold upon your head,"
They answered altogether:
"Buy from us with a golden curl."
She clipped a precious golden lock,
She dropped a tear more rare than pearl,
Then sucked their fruit globes fair or red:
Sweeter than honey from the rock,
Stronger than man-rejoicing wine,
Clearer than water flowed that juice;
She never tasted such before,
How should it cloy with length of use?
She sucked and sucked and sucked the more
Fruits which that unknown orchard bore,
She sucked until her lips were sore;
Then flung the emptied rinds away,
But gathered up one kernel stone,
And knew not was it night or day
As she turned home alone.

Lizzie met her at the gate
Full of wise upbraidings:
"Dear, you should not stay so late,
Twilight is not good for maidens;
Should not loiter in the glen
In the haunts of goblin men.
Do you not remember Jeanie,
How she met them in the moonlight,
Took their gifts both choice and many,
Ate their fruits and wore their flowers
Plucked from bowers
Where summer ripens at all hours?
But ever in the moonlight
She pined and pined away;
Sought them by night and day,
Found them no more, but dwindled and grew gray;
Then fell with the first snow,
While to this day no grass will grow
Where she lies low:
I planted daisies there a year ago
That never blow.
You should not loiter so."
"Nay hush," said Laura.
"Nay hush, my sister:
I ate and ate my fill,
Yet my mouth waters still;
To-morrow night I will
Buy more," and kissed her.
"Have done with sorrow;
I'll bring you plums to-morrow
Fresh on their mother twigs,
Cherries worth getting;
You cannot think what figs
My teeth have met in,
What melons, icy-cold
Piled on a dish of gold
Too huge for me to hold,
What peaches with a velvet nap,
Pellucid grapes without one seed:
Odorous indeed must be the mead
Whereon they grow, and pure the wave they drink,
With lilies at the brink,
And sugar-sweet their sap."

Golden head by golden head,
Like two pigeons in one nest
Folded in each other's wings,
They lay down, in their curtained bed:
Like two blossoms on one stem,
Like two flakes of new-fallen snow,

Like two wands of ivory
Tipped with gold for awful kings.
Moon and stars beamed in at them,
Wind sang to them lullaby,
Lumbering owls forbore to fly,
Not a bat flapped to and fro
Round their rest:
Cheek to cheek and breast to breast
Locked together in one nest.

Early in the morning
When the first cock crowed his warning,
Neat like bees, as sweet and busy,
Laura rose with Lizzie:
Fetched in honey, milked the cows,
Aired and set to rights the house,
Kneaded cakes of whitest wheat,
Cakes for dainty mouths to eat,
Next churned butter, whipped up cream,
Fed their poultry, sat and sewed;
Talked as modest maidens should
Lizzie with an open heart,
Laura in an absent dream,
One content, one sick in part;
One warbling for the mere bright day's delight,
One longing for the night.

At length slow evening came
They went with pitchers to the reedy brook;
Lizzie most placid in her look,
Laura most like a leaping flame.
They drew the gurgling water from its deep
Lizzie plucked purple and rich golden flags,
Then turning homeward said: "The sunset flushes
Those furthest loftiest crags;
Come, Laura, not another maiden lags,
No wilful squirrel wags,
The beasts and birds are fast asleep."
But Laura loitered still among the rushes
And said the bank was steep.

And said the hour was early still,
The dew not fallen, the wind not chill:
Listening ever, but not catching
The customary cry,
"Come buy, come buy,"
With its iterated jingle
Of sugar-baited words:
Not for all her watching
Once discerning even one goblin
Racing, whisking, tumbling, hobbling;

Let alone the herds
That used to tramp along the glen,
In groups or single,
Of brisk fruit-merchant men.

Till Lizzie urged, "O Laura, come,
I hear the fruit-call, but I dare not look:
You should not loiter longer at this brook:
Come with me home.
The stars rise, the moon bends her arc,
Each glow-worm winks her spark,
Let us get home before the night grows dark;
For clouds may gather even
Though this is summer weather,
Put out the lights and drench us through;
Then if we lost our way what should we do?"

Laura turned cold as stone
To find her sister heard that cry alone,
That goblin cry,
"Come buy our fruits, come buy."
Must she then buy no more such dainty fruit?
Must she no more such succous pasture find,
Gone deaf and blind?
Her tree of life drooped from the root:
She said not one word in her heart's sore ache;
But peering thro' the dimness, naught discerning,
Trudged home, her pitcher dripping all the way;
So crept to bed, and lay
Silent 'til Lizzie slept;
Then sat up in a passionate yearning,
And gnashed her teeth for balked desire, and wept
As if her heart would break.

Day after day, night after night,
Laura kept watch in vain,
In sullen silence of exceeding pain.
She never caught again the goblin cry:
"Come buy, come buy,"
She never spied the goblin men
Hawking their fruits along the glen:
But when the noon waxed bright
Her hair grew thin and gray;
She dwindled, as the fair full moon doth turn
To swift decay, and burn
Her fire away.

One day remembering her kernel-stone
She set it by a wall that faced the south;
Dewed it with tears, hoped for a root,
Watched for a waxing shoot,

But there came none;
It never saw the sun,
It never felt the trickling moisture run:
While with sunk eyes and faded mouth
She dreamed of melons, as a traveller sees
False waves in desert drouth
With shade of leaf-crowned trees,
And burns the thirstier in the sandful breeze.

She no more swept the house,
Tended the fowls or cows,
Fetched honey, kneaded cakes of wheat,
Brought water from the brook:
But sat down listless in the chimney-nook
And would not eat.

Tender Lizzie could not bear
To watch her sister's cankerous care,
Yet not to share.
She night and morning
Caught the goblins' cry:
"Come buy our orchard fruits,
Come buy, come buy."
Beside the brook, along the glen
She heard the tramp of goblin men,
The voice and stir
Poor Laura could not hear;
Longed to buy fruit to comfort her,
But feared to pay too dear.

She thought of Jeanie in her grave,
Who should have been a bride;
But who for joys brides hope to have
Fell sick and died
In her gay prime,
In earliest winter-time,
With the first glazing rime,
With the first snow-fall of crisp winter-time.

Till Laura, dwindling,
Seemed knocking at Death's door:
Then Lizzie weighed no more
Better and worse,
But put a silver penny in her purse,
Kissed Laura, crossed the heath with clumps of furze
At twilight, halted by the brook,
And for the first time in her life
Began to listen and look.

Laughed every goblin
When they spied her peeping:

Came towards her hobbling,
Flying, running, leaping,
Puffing and blowing,
Chuckling, clapping, crowing,
Clucking and gobbling,
Mopping and mowing,
Full of airs and graces,
Pulling wry faces,
Demure grimaces,
Cat-like and rat-like,
Ratel and wombat-like,
Snail-paced in a hurry,
Parrot-voiced and whistler,
Helter-skelter, hurry-skurry,
Chattering like magpies,
Fluttering like pigeons,
Gliding like fishes,
Hugged her and kissed her;
Squeezed and caressed her;
Stretched up their dishes,
Panniers and plates:
"Look at our apples
Russet and dun,
Bob at our cherries
Bite at our peaches,
Citrons and dates,
Grapes for the asking,
Pears red with basking
Out in the sun,
Plums on their twigs;
Pluck them and suck them,
Pomegranates, figs."

"Good folk," said Lizzie,
Mindful of Jeanie,
"Give me much and many";
Held out her apron,
Tossed them her penny.
"Nay, take a seat with us,
Honor and eat with us,"
They answered grinning;
"Our feast is but beginning.
Night yet is early,
Warm and dew-pearly,
Wakeful and starry:
Such fruits as these
No man can carry;
Half their bloom would fly,
Half their dew would dry,
Half their flavor would pass by.
Sit down and feast with us,

Be welcome guest with us,
Cheer you and rest with us."
"Thank you," said Lizzie; "but one waits
At home alone for me:
So, without further parleying,
If you will not sell me any
Of your fruits though much and many,
Give me back my silver penny
I tossed you for a fee."
They began to scratch their pates,
No longer wagging, purring,
But visibly demurring,
Grunting and snarling.
One called her proud,
Cross-grained, uncivil;
Their tones waxed loud,
Their looks were evil.
Lashing their tails
They trod and hustled her,
Elbowed and jostled her,
Clawed with their nails,
Barking, mewing, hissing, mocking,
Tore her gown and soiled her stocking,
Twitched her hair out by the roots,
Stamped upon her tender feet,
Held her hands and squeezed their fruits
Against her mouth to make her eat.

White and golden Lizzie stood,
Like a lily in a flood,
Like a rock of blue-veined stone
Lashed by tides obstreperously,
Like a beacon left alone
In a hoary roaring sea,
Sending up a golden fire,
Like a fruit-crowned orange-tree
White with blossoms honey-sweet
Sore beset by wasp and bee,
Like a royal virgin town
Topped with gilded dome and spire
Close beleaguered by a fleet
Mad to tear her standard down.

One may lead a horse to water,
Twenty cannot make him drink.
Though the goblins cuffed and caught her,
Coaxed and fought her,
Bullied and besought her,
Scratched her, pinched her black as ink,
Kicked and knocked her,
Mauled and mocked her,

Lizzie uttered not a word;
Would not open lip from lip
Lest they should cram a mouthful in;
But laughed in heart to feel the drip
Of juice that syruped all her face,
And lodged in dimples of her chin,
And streaked her neck which quaked like curd.
At last the evil people,
Worn out by her resistance,
Flung back her penny, kicked their fruit
Along whichever road they took,
Not leaving root or stone or shoot.
Some writhed into the ground,
Some dived into the brook
With ring and ripple.
Some scudded on the gale without a sound,
Some vanished in the distance.

In a smart, ache, tingle,
Lizzie went her way;
Knew not was it night or day;
Sprang up the bank, tore through the furze,
Threaded copse and dingle,
And heard her penny jingle
Bouncing in her purse,
Its bounce was music to her ear.
She ran and ran
As if she feared some goblin man
Dogged her with gibe or curse
Or something worse:
But not one goblin skurried after,
Nor was she pricked by fear;
The kind heart made her windy-paced
That urged her home quite out of breath with haste
And inward laughter.

She cried "Laura," up the garden,
"Did you miss me?
Come and kiss me.
Never mind my bruises,
Hug me, kiss me, suck my juices
Squeezed from goblin fruits for you,
Goblin pulp and goblin dew.
Eat me, drink me, love me;
Laura, make much of me:
For your sake I have braved the glen
And had to do with goblin merchant men."

Laura started from her chair,
Flung her arms up in the air,
Clutched her hair:

"Lizzie, Lizzie, have you tasted
For my sake the fruit forbidden?
Must your light like mine be hidden,
Your young life like mine be wasted,
Undone in mine undoing,
And ruined in my ruin;
Thirsty, cankered, goblin-ridden?"
She clung about her sister,
Kissed and kissed and kissed her:
Tears once again
Refreshed her shrunken eyes,
Dropping like rain
After long sultry drouth;
Shaking with aguish fear, and pain,
She kissed and kissed her with a hungry mouth.

Her lips began to scorch,
That juice was wormwood to her tongue,
She loathed the feast:
Writhing as one possessed she leaped and sung,
Rent all her robe, and wrung
Her hands in lamentable haste,
And beat her breast.
Her locks streamed like the torch
Borne by a racer at full speed,
Or like the mane of horses in their flight,
Or like an eagle when she stems the light
Straight toward the sun,
Or like a caged thing freed,
Or like a flying flag when armies run.

Swift fire spread through her veins, knocked at her heart,
Met the fire smouldering there
And overbore its lesser flame,
She gorged on bitterness without a name:
Ah! fool, to choose such part
Of soul-consuming care!
Sense failed in the mortal strife:
Like the watch-tower of a town
Which an earthquake shatters down,
Like a lightning-stricken mast,
Like a wind-uprooted tree
Spun about,
Like a foam-topped water-spout
Cast down headlong in the sea,
She fell at last;
Pleasure past and anguish past,
Is it death or is it life ?

Life out of death.
That night long Lizzie watched by her,

Counted her pulse's flagging stir,
Felt for her breath,
Held water to her lips, and cooled her face
With tears and fanning leaves:
But when the first birds chirped about their eaves,
And early reapers plodded to the place
Of golden sheaves,
And dew-wet grass
Bowed in the morning winds so brisk to pass,
And new buds with new day
Opened of cup-like lilies on the stream,
Laura awoke as from a dream,
Laughed in the innocent old way,
Hugged Lizzie but not twice or thrice;
Her gleaming locks showed not one thread of gray,
Her breath was sweet as May,
And light danced in her eyes.

Days, weeks, months, years
Afterwards, when both were wives
With children of their own;
Their mother-hearts beset with fears,
Their lives bound up in tender lives;
Laura would call the little ones
And tell them of her early prime,
Those pleasant days long gone
Of not-returning time:
Would talk about the haunted glen,
The wicked, quaint fruit-merchant men,
Their fruits like honey to the throat,
But poison in the blood;
(Men sell not such in any town)
Would tell them how her sister stood
In deadly peril to do her good,
And win the fiery antidote:
Then joining hands to little hands
Would bid them cling together,
"For there is no friend like a sister,
In calm or stormy weather,
To cheer one on the tedious way,
To fetch one if one goes astray,
To lift one if one totters down,
To strengthen whilst one stands."

A BIRTHDAY

My heart is like a singing bird
Whose nest is in a water'd shoot;
My heart is like an apple-tree
Whose boughs are bent with thickset fruit;
My heart is like a rainbow shell

That paddles in a halcyon sea;
My heart is gladder than all these
Because my love is come to me.

Raise me a dais of silk and down;
Hang it with vair and purple dyes;
Carve it in doves and pomegranates,
And peacocks with a hundred eyes;
Work it in gold and silver grapes,
In leaves and silver fleurs-de-lys;
Because the birthday of my life
Is come, my love is come to me.

DREAMLAND
Where sunless rivers weep
Their waves into the deep,
She sleeps a charmed sleep:
Awake her not.
Led by a single star,
She came from very far
To seek where shadows are
Her pleasant lot.

She left the rosy morn,
She left the fields of corn,
For twilight cold and lorn
And water springs.
Through sleep, as through a veil,
She sees the sky look pale,
And hears the nightingale
That sadly sings.

Rest, rest, a perfect rest
Shed over brow and breast;
Her face is toward the west,
The purple land.
She cannot see the grain
Ripening on hill and plain;
She cannot feel the rain
Upon her hand.

Rest, rest, for evermore
Upon a mossy shore;
Rest, rest at the heart's core
Till time shall cease:
Sleep that no pain shall wake;
Night that no morn shall break
Till joy shall overtake
Her perfect peace.

ECHO

Come to me in the silence of the night;
Come in the speaking silence of a dream;
Come with soft rounded cheeks and eyes as bright
As sunlight on a stream;
Come back in tears,
O memory, hope, love of finished years.

O dream how sweet, too sweet, too bitter sweet,
Whose wakening should have been in Paradise,
Where souls brimfull of love abide and meet;
Where thirsting longing eyes
Watch the slow door
That opening, letting in, lets out no more.

Yet come to me in dreams, that I may live
My very life again though cold in death:
Come back to me in dreams, that I may give
Pulse for pulse, breath for breath:
Speak low, lean low
As long ago, my love, how long ago.

FROG & TOAD

Hopping frog, hop here and be seen,
I'll not pelt you with stick or stone:
Your cap is laced and your coat is green;
Good bye, we'll let each other alone.

Plodding toad, plod here and be looked at,
You the finger of scorn is crooked at:
But though you're lumpish, you're harmless too;
You won't hurt me, and I won't hurt you.

IF A MOUSE COULD FLY

If a mouse could fly,
Or if a crow could swim,
Or if a sprat could walk and talk,
I'd like to be like him.
If a mouse could fly,
He might fly away;
Or if a crow could swim,
It might turn him grey;
Or if a sprat could walk and talk,
What would he find to say?

THE CITY MOUSE AND THE COUNTRY MOUSE

The city mouse lives in a house;

The garden mouse lives in a bower,
He's friendly with the frogs and toads,
And sees the pretty plants in flower.

The city mouse eats bread and cheese; -
The garden mouse eats what he can;
We will not grudge him seeds and stalks,
Poor little timid furry man.

A HOPE CAROL
A Hope Carol
A night was near, a day was near,
Between a day and night
I heard sweet voices calling clear,
Calling me:
I heard a whirr of wing on wing,
But could not see the sight;
I long to see my birds that sing,
I long to see.
Below the stars, beyond the moon,
Between the night and day
I heard a rising falling tune
Calling me:
I long to see the pipes and strings
Whereon such minstrels play;
I long to see each face that sings,
I long to see.
Today or may be not today,
Tonight or not tonight,
All voices that command or pray
Calling me,
Shall kindle in my soul such fire
And in my eyes such light
That I shall see that heart's desire
I long to see.

IN THE WILLOW SHADE
I sat beneath a willow tree,
Where water falls and calls;
While fancies upon fancies solaced me,
Some true, and some were false.

Who set their heart upon a hope
That never comes to pass,
Droop in the end like fading heliotrope
The sun's wan looking-glass.

Who set their will upon a whim
Clung to through good and ill,

Are wrecked alike whether they sink or swim,
Or hit or miss their will.

All things are vain that wax and wane,
For which we waste our breath;
Love only doth not wane and is not vain,
Love only outlives death.

A singing lark rose toward the sky,
Circling he sang amain;
He sang, a speck scarce visible sky-high,
And then he sank again.

A second like a sunlit spark
Flashed singing up his track;
But never overtook that foremost lark,
And songless fluttered back.

A hovering melody of birds
Haunted the air above;
They clearly sang contentment without words,
And youth and joy and love.

O silvery weeping willow tree
With all leaves shivering,
Have you no purpose but to shadow me
Beside this rippled spring?

On this first fleeting day of Spring,
For Winter is gone by,
And every bird on every quivering wing
Floats in a sunny sky;

On this first Summer-like soft day,
While sunshine steeps the air,
And every cloud has gat itself away,
And birds sing everywhere.

Have you no purpose in the world
But thus to shadow me
With all your tender drooping twigs unfurled,
O weeping willow tree?

With all your tremulous leaves outspread
Betwixt me and the sun,
While here I loiter on a mossy bed
With half my work undone;

My work undone, that should be done
At once with all my might;
For after the long day and lingering sun

Comes the unworking night.

This day is lapsing on its way,
Is lapsing out of sight;
And after all the chances of the day
Comes the resourceless night.

The weeping willow shook its head
And stretched its shadow long;
The west grew crimson, the sun smoldered red,
The birds forbore a song.

Slow wind sighed through the willow leaves,
The ripple made a moan,
The world drooped murmuring like a thing that grieves;
And then I felt alone.

I rose to go, and felt the chill,
And shivered as I went;
Yet shivering wondered, and I wonder still,
What more that willow meant;

That silvery weeping willow tree
With all leaves shivering,
Which spent one long day overshadowing me
Beside a spring in Spring.

SUMMER
Winter is cold-hearted
Spring is yea and nay,
Autumn is a weather-cock
Blown every way:
Summer days for me
When every leaf is on its tree;

When Robin's not a beggar,
And Jenny Wren's a bride,
And larks hang singing, singing, singing,
Over the wheat-fields wide,
And anchored lilies ride,
And the pendulum spider
Swings from side to side,

And blue-black beetles transact business,
And gnats fly in a host,
And furry caterpillars hasten
That no time be lost,
And moths grow fat and thrive,
And ladybirds arrive.

Before green apples blush,
Before green nuts embrown,
Why, one day in the country
Is worth a month in town;
Is worth a day and a year
Of the dusty, musty, lag-last fashion
That days drone elsewhere.

SUMMER IS ENDED
To think that this meaningless thing was ever a rose,
Scentless, colourless, this!
Will it ever be thus (who knows?)
Thus with our bliss,
If we wait till the close?

Though we care not to wait for the end, there comes the end
Sooner, later, at last,
Which nothing can mar, nothing mend:
An end locked fast,
Bent we cannot re-bend.

AN OCTOBER GARDEN
In my Autumn garden I was fain
To mourn among my scattered roses;
Alas for that last rosebud which uncloses
To Autumn's languid sun and rain
When all the world is on the wane!
Which has not felt the sweet constraint of June,
Nor heard the nightingale in tune.

Broad-faced asters by my garden walk,
You are but coarse compared with roses:
More choice, more dear that rosebud which uncloses
Faint-scented, pinched, upon its stalk,
That least and last which cold winds balk;
A rose it is though least and last of all,
A rose to me though at the fall.

CHRISTMAS EVE
Christmas hath a darkness
Brighter than the blazing noon,
Christmas hath a chillness
Warmer than the heat of June,
Christmas hath a beauty
Lovelier than the world can show:
For Christmas bringeth Jesus,
Brought for us so low.

Earth, strike up your music,
Birds that sing and bells that ring;
Heaven hath answring music
For all Angels soon to sing:
Earth, put on your whitest
Bridal robe of spotless snow:
For Christmas bringeth Jesus,
Brought for us so low.

GOOD FRIDAY
Am I a stone and not a sheep
That I can stand, O Christ, beneath Thy Cross,
To number drop by drop Thy Blood's slow loss,
And yet not weep?

Not so those women loved
Who with exceeding grief lamented Thee;
Not so fallen Peter weeping bitterly;
Not so the thief was moved;

Not so the Sun and Moon
Which hid their faces in a starless sky,
A horror of great darkness at broad noon—
I, only I.

Yet give not o'er,
But seek Thy sheep, true Shepherd of the flock;
Greater than Moses, turn and look once more
And smite a rock.

A YEARS WINDFALLS
On the wind of January
Down flits the snow,
Travelling from the frozen North
As cold as it can blow.
Poor robin redbreast,
Look where he comes;
Let him in to feel your fire,
And toss him of your crumbs.

On the wind in February
Snowflakes float still,
Half inclined to turn to rain,
Nipping, dripping, chill.
Then the thaws swell the streams,
And swollen rivers swell the sea:
If the winter ever ends
How pleasant it will be!

In the wind of windy March
The catkins drop down,
Curly, caterpillar-like,
Curious green and brown.
With concourse of nest-building birds
And leaf-buds by the way,
We begin to think of flowers
And life and nuts some day.

With the gusts of April
Rich fruit-tree blossoms fall,
On the hedged-in orchard-green,
From the southern wall.
Apple-trees and pear-trees
Shed petals white or pink,
Plum-trees and peach-trees;
While sharp showers sink and sink.

Little brings the May breeze
Beside pure scent of flowers,
While all things wax and nothing wanes
In lengthening daylight hours.
Across the hyacinth beds
The wind lags warm and sweet,
Across the hawthorn tops,
Across the blades of wheat.

In the wind of sunny June
Thrives the red rose crop,
Every day fresh blossoms blow
While the first leaves drop;
White rose and yellow rose
And moss-rose choice to find,
And the cottage cabbage-rose
Not one whit behind.

On the blast of scorched July
Drives the pelting hail,
From thunderous lightning-clouds, that blot
Blue heaven grown lurid-pale.
Weedy waves are tossed ashore,
Sea-things strange to sight
Gasp upon the barren shore
And fade away in light.

In the parching August wind
Corn-fields bow the head,
Sheltered in round valley depths,
On low hills outspread.
Early leaves drop loitering down
Weightless on the breeze,

First fruits of the year's decay
From the withering trees.

In brisk wind of September
The heavy-headed fruits
Shake upon their bending boughs
And drop from the shoots;
Some glow golden in the sun,
Some show green and streaked,
Some set forth a purple bloom,
Some blush rosy-cheeked.

In strong blast of October
At the equinox,
Stirred up in his hollow bed
Broad ocean rocks;
Plunge the ships on his bosom,
Leaps and plunges the foam,—
It's oh! for mothers' sons at sea,
That they were safe at home.

In slack wind of November
The fog forms and shifts;
All the world comes out again
When the fog lifts.
Loosened from their sapless twigs
Leaves drop with every gust;
Drifting, rustling, out of sight
In the damp or dust.

Last of all, December,
The year's sands nearly run,
Speeds on the shortest day,
Curtails the sun;
With its bleak raw wind
Lays the last leaves low,
Brings back the nightly frosts,
Brings back the snow.

HOW MANY SECONDS IN A MINUTE
How many seconds in a minute?
Sixty, and no more in it.
How many minutes in an hour?
Sixty for sun and shower.
How many hours in a day?
Twenty-four for work and play.
How many days in a week?
Seven both to hear and speak.
How many weeks in a month?
Four, as the swift moon runneth.

How many months in a year?
Twelve the almanack makes clear.
How many years in an age?
One hundred says the sage.
How many ages in time?
No one knows the rhyme.

WHO HAS SEEN THE WIND
Who has seen the wind?
Neither I nor you.
But when the leaves hang trembling,
The wind is passing through.
Who has seen the wind?
Neither you nor I.
But when the trees bow down their heads,
The wind is passing by.

AN EMERALD IS AS GREEN AS GREEN
An emerald is as green as grass;
A ruby red as blood;
A sapphire shines as blue as heaven;
A flint lies in the mud.
A diamond is a brilliant stone,
To catch the world's desire;
An opal holds a fiery spark;
But a flint holds fire.

IN THE BLEAK MIDWINTER
In the bleak midwinter, frosty wind made moan,
Earth stood hard as iron, water like a stone;
Snow had fallen, snow on snow, snow on snow,
In the bleak midwinter, long ago.

Our God, Heaven cannot hold Him, nor earth sustain;
Heaven and earth shall flee away when He comes to reign.
In the bleak midwinter a stable place sufficed
The Lord God Almighty, Jesus Christ.

Enough for Him, Whom cherubim, worship night and day,
Breastful of milk, and a mangerful of hay;
Enough for Him, Whom angels fall before,
The ox and ass and camel which adore.

Angels and archangels may have gathered there,
Cherubim and seraphim thronged the air;
But His mother only, in her maiden bliss,
Worshipped the beloved with a kiss.

What can I give Him, poor as I am?
If I were a shepherd, I would bring a lamb;
If I were a Wise Man, I would do my part;
Yet what I can I give Him: give my heart.

WINTER – MY SECRET

I tell my secret? No indeed, not I:
Perhaps some day, who knows?
But not today; it froze, and blows, and snows,
And you're too curious: fie!
You want to hear it? well:
Only, my secret's mine, and I won't tell.

Or, after all, perhaps there's none:
Suppose there is no secret after all,
But only just my fun.
Today's a nipping day, a biting day;
In which one wants a shawl,
A veil, a cloak, and other wraps:
I cannot ope to every one who taps,
And let the draughts come whistling thro' my hall;
Come bounding and surrounding me,
Come buffeting, astounding me,
Nipping and clipping thro' my wraps and all.
I wear my mask for warmth: who ever shows
His nose to Russian snows
To be pecked at by every wind that blows?
You would not peck? I thank you for good will,
Believe, but leave that truth untested still.

Spring's and expansive time: yet I don't trust
March with its peck of dust,
Nor April with its rainbow-crowned brief showers,
Nor even May, whose flowers
One frost may wither thro' the sunless hours.
Perhaps some languid summer day,
When drowsy birds sing less and less,
And golden fruit is ripening to excess,
If there's not too much sun nor too much cloud,
And the warm wind is neither still nor loud,
Perhaps my secret I may say,
Or you may guess.

JANUARY COLD DESOLATE

January cold desolate;
February all dripping wet;
March wind ranges;
April changes;
Birds sing in tune

To flowers of May,
And sunny June
Brings longest day;
In scorched July
The storm-clouds fly
Lightning-torn;
August bears corn,
September fruit;
In rough October
Earth must disrobe her;
Stars fall and shoot
In keen November;
And night is long
And cold is strong
In bleak December.

AFTER THIS JUDGEMENT
As eager homebound traveller to the goal,
Or steadfast seeker on an unsearched main,
Or martyr panting for an aureole,
My fellow-pilgrims pass me, and attain
That hidden mansion of perpetual peace
Where keen desire and hope dwell free from pain:
That gate stands open of perennial ease;
I view the glory till I partly long,
Yet lack the fire of love which quickens these.
O passing Angel, speed me with a song,
A melody of heaven to reach my heart
And rouse me to the race and make me strong;
Till in such music I take up my part
Swelling those Hallelujahs full of rest,
One, tenfold, hundredfold, with heavenly art,
Fulfilling north and south and east and west,
Thousand, ten thousandfold, innumerable,
All blent in one yet each one manifest;
Each one distinguished and beloved as well
As if no second voice in earth or heaven
Were lifted up the Love of God to tell.
Ah, Love of God, which Thine own Self hast given
To me most poor, and made me rich in love,
Love that dost pass the tenfold seven times seven,
Draw Thou mine eyes, draw Thou my heart above,
My treasure ad my heart store Thou in Thee,
Brood over me with yearnings of a dove;
Be Husband, Brother, closest Friend to me;
Love me as very mother loves her son,
Her sucking firstborn fondled on her knee:
Yea, more than mother loves her little one;
For, earthly, even a mother may forget
And feel no pity for its piteous moan;

But thou, O Love of God, remember yet,
Through the dry desert, through the waterflood
(Life, death) until the Great White Throne is set.
If now I am sick in chewing the bitter cud
Of sweet past sin, though solaced by Thy grace
And ofttimes strengthened by Thy Flesh and Blood,
How shall I then stand up before Thy face
When from Thine eyes repentance shall be hid
And utmost Justice stand in Mercy's place:
When every sin I thought or spoke or did
Shall meet me at the inexorable bar,
And there be no man standing in the mid
To plead for me; while star fallen after star
With heaven and earth are like a ripened shock,
And all time's mighty works and wonders are
Consumed as in a moment; when no rock
Remains to fall on me, no tree to hide,
But I stand all creation's gazing-stock
Exposed and comfortless on every side,
Placed trembling in the final balances
Whose poise this hour, this moment, must be tried?—
Ah Love of God, if greater love than this
Hath no man, that a man die for his friend,
And if such love of love Thine Own Love is,
Plead with Thyself, with me, before the end;
Redeem me from the irrevocable past;
Pitch Thou Thy Presence round me to defend;
Yea seek with pierced feet, yea hold me fast
With pierced hands whose wounds were made by love;
Not what I am, remember what Thou wast
When darkness hid from Thee Thy heavens above,
And sin Thy Father's Face, while thou didst drink
The bitter cup of death, didst taste thereof
For every man; while Thou wast nigh to sink
Beneath the intense intolerable rod,
Grown sick of love; not what I am, but think
Thy Life then ransomed mine, my God, my God.

AFTER DEATH

The curtains were half drawn, the floor was swept
And strewn with rushes, rosemary and may
Lay thick upon the bed on which I lay,
Where through the lattice ivy-shadows crept.
He leaned above me, thinking that I slept
And could not hear him; but I heard him say:
'Poor child, poor child:' and as he turned away
Came a deep silence, and I knew he wept.
He did not touch the shroud, or raise the fold
That hid my face, or take my hand in his,
Or ruffle the smooth pillows for my head:

He did not love me living; but once dead
He pitied me; and very sweet it is
To know he still is warm though I am cold.

DEAD BEFORE DEATH

Ah! changed and cold, how changed and very cold,
With stiffened smiling lips and cold calm eyes:
Changed, yet the same; much knowing, little wise;
This was the promise of the days of old!
Grown hard and stubborn in the ancient mould,
Grown rigid in the sham of lifelong lies:
We hoped for better things as years would rise,
But it is over as a tale once told.
All fallen the blossom that no fruitage bore,
All lost the present and the future time,
All lost, all lost, the lapse that went before:
So lost till death shut-to the opened door,
So lost from chime to everlasting chime,
So cold and lost for ever evermore.

LIFE AND DEATH

Life is not sweet. One day it will be sweet
To shut our eyes and die:
Nor feel the wild flowers blow, nor birds dart by
With flitting butterfly,
Nor grass grow long above our heads and feet,
Nor hear the happy lark that soars sky high,
Nor sigh that spring is fleet and summer fleet,
Nor mark the waxing wheat,
Nor know who sits in our accustomed seat.

Life is not good. One day it will be good
To die, then live again;
To sleep meanwhile: so not to feel the wane
Of shrunk leaves dropping in the wood,
Nor hear the foamy lashing of the main,
Nor mark the blackened bean-fields, nor where stood
Rich ranks of golden grain
Only dead refuse stubble clothe the plain:
Asleep from risk, asleep from pain.

REMEMBER

Remember me when I am gone away,
Gone far away into the silent land;
When you can no more hold me by the hand,
Nor I half turn to go yet turning stay.
Remember me when no more day by day
You tell me of our future that you plann'd:

Only remember me; you understand
It will be late to counsel then or pray.
Yet if you should forget me for a while
And afterwards remember, do not grieve:
For if the darkness and corruption leave
A vestige of the thoughts that once I had,
Better by far you should forget and smile
Than that you should remember and be sad.

A BETTER RESURRECTION
I have no wit, no words, no tears;
My heart within me like a stone
Is numbed too much for hopes or fears.
Look right, look left, I dwell alone;
I lift mine eyes, but dimmed with grief
No everlasting hills I see;
My life is in the falling leaf:
O Jesus, quicken me.
My life is like a faded leaf,
My harvest dwindled to a husk:
Truly my life is void and brief
And tedious in the barren dusk;
My life is like a frozen thing,
No bud nor greenness can I see:
Yet rise it shall - the sap of spring;
O Jesus, rise in me.
My life is like a broken bowl,
A broken bowl that cannot hold
One drop of water for my soul
Or cordial in the searching cold;
Cast in the fire the perished thing;
Melt and remould it, till it be
A royal cup for Him, my King:
O Jesus, drink of me.

DE PROFUNDIS
Oh why is heaven built so far,
Oh why is earth set so remote?
I cannot reach the nearest star
That hangs afloat.

I would not care to reach the moon,
One round monotonous of change;
Yet even she repeats her tune
Beyond my range.

I never watch the scattered fire
Of stars, or sun's far-trailing train,
But all my heart is one desire,

And all in vain:

For I am bound with fleshly bands,
Joy, beauty, lie beyond my scope;
I strain my heart, I stretch my hands,
And catch at hope.

DREAM LAND
Where sunless rivers weep
Their waves into the deep,
She sleeps a charmèd sleep:
Awake her not.
Led by a single star,
She came from very far
To seek where shadows are
Her pleasant lot.

She left the rosy morn,
She left the fields of corn,
For twilight cold and lorn
And water springs.
Through sleep, as through a veil,
She sees the sky look pale,
And hears the nightingale
That sadly sings.

Rest, rest, a perfect rest
Shed over brow and breast;
Her face is toward the west,
The purple land.
She cannot see the grain
Ripening on hill and plain;
She cannot feel the rain
Upon her hand.

Rest, rest, for evermore
Upon a mossy shore;
Rest, rest at the heart's core
Till time shall cease:
Sleep that no pain shall wake;
Night that no morn shall break
Till joy shall overtake
Her perfect peace.

PASSING AWAY, SAITH THE WORLD
Passing away, saith the World, passing away:
Chances, beauty and youth, sapped day by day:
Thy life never continueth in one stay.
Is the eye waxen dim, is the dark hair changing to grey

That hath won neither laurel nor bay?
I shall clothe myself in Spring and bud in May:
Thou, root-stricken, shalt not rebuild thy decay
On my bosom for aye.
Then I answer'd: Yea.

Passing away, saith my Soul, passing away:
With its burden of fear and hope, of labour and play,
Hearken what the past doth witness and say:
Rust in thy gold, a moth is in thine array,
A canker is in thy bud, thy leaf must decay.
At midnight, at cockcrow, at morning, one certain day
Lo, the Bridegroom shall come and shall not delay:
Watch thou and pray.
Then I answer'd: Yea.

Passing away, saith my God, passing away:
Winter passeth after the long delay:
New grapes on the vine, new figs on the tender spray,
Turtle calleth turtle in Heaven's May.
Though I tarry, wait for Me, trust Me, watch and pray.
Arise, come away, night is past and lo it is day,
My love, My sister, My spouse, thou shalt hear Me say.
Then I answer'd: Yea.

THE CONVENT THRESHOLD
There's blood between us, love, my love,
There's father's blood, there's brother's blood,
And blood's a bar I cannot pass.
I choose the stairs that mount above,
Stair after golden sky-ward stair,
To city and to sea of glass.
My lily feet are soiled with mud,
With scarlet mud which tells a tale
Of hope that was, of guilt that was,
Of love that shall not yet avail;
Alas, my heart, if I could bare
My heart, this selfsame stain is there:
I seek the sea of glass and fire
To wash the spot, to burn the snare;
Lo, stairs are meant to lift us higher -
Mount with me, mount the kindled stair.

Your eyes look earthward, mine look up.
I see the far-off city grand,
Beyond the hills a watered land,
Beyond the gulf a gleaming strand
Of mansions where the righteous sup,
Who sleep at ease among their trees,
Or wake to sing a cadenced hymn

With Cherubim and Seraphim;
They bore the Cross, they drained the cup,
Racked, roasted, crushed, wrenched limb from limb,
They the offscouring of the world.
The heaven of starry heavens unfurled,
The sun before their face is dim.
You looking earthward, what see you?
Milk-white, wine-flushed among the vines,
Up and down leaping, to and fro,
Most glad, most full, made strong with wines,
Blooming as peaches pearled with dew,
Their golden windy hair afloat,
Love-music warbling in their throat,
Young men and women come and go.

You linger, yet the time is short:
Flee for your life, gird up your strength
To flee; the shadows stretched at length
Show that day wanes, that night draws nigh;
Flee to the mountain, tarry not.
Is this a time for smile and sigh,
For songs among the secret trees
Where sudden blue birds nest and sport?
The time is short and yet you stay:
To-day, while it is called to-day,
Kneel, wrestle, knock, do violence, pray;
To-day is short, to-morrow nigh:
Why will you die? why will you die?

You sinned with me a pleasant sin:
Repent with me, for I repent.
Woe's me the lore I must unlearn!
Woe's me that easy way we went,
So rugged when I would return!
How long until my sleep begin
How long shall stretch these nights and days?
Surely, clean Angels cry, she prays;
She laves her soul with tedious tears:
How long must stretch these years and years?

I turn from you my cheeks and eyes,
My hair which you shall see no more -
Alas for joy that went before,
For joy that dies, for love that dies.
Only my lips still turn to you,
My livid lips that cry, Repent.
O weary life, O weary Lent,
O weary time whose stars are few.

How shall I rest in Paradise,
Or sit on steps of heaven alone

If Saints and Angels spoke of love
Should I not answer from my throne:
Have pity upon me, ye my friends,
For I have heard the sound thereof:
Should I not turn with yearning eyes,
Turn earthwards with a pitiful pang?
Oh save me from a pang in heaven.
By all the gifts we took and gave,
Repent, repent, and be forgiven:
This life is long, but yet it ends;
Repent and purge your soul and save:
No gladder song the morning stars
Upon their birthday morning sang
Than Angels sing when one repents.

I tell you what I dreamed last night:
A spirit with transfigured face
Fire-footed clomb an infinite space.
I heard his hundred pinions clang,
Heaven-bells rejoicing rang and rang,
Heaven-air was thrilled with subtle scents,
Worlds spun upon their rushing cars.
He mounted, shrieking, Give me light!
Still light was poured on him, more light;
Angels, Archangels he outstripped,
Exulting in exceeding might,
And trod the skirts of Cherubim.
Still Give me light, he shrieked; and dipped
His thirsty face, and drank a sea,
Athirst with thirst it could not slake.
I saw him, drunk with knowledge, take
From aching brows the aureole crown
His locks writhe like a cloven snake
He left his throne to grovel down
And lick the dust of Seraphs' feet;
For what is knowledge duly weighed?
Knowledge is strong, but love is sweet;
Yea, all the progress he had made
Was but to learn that all is small
Save love, for love is all in all.

I tell you what I dreamed last night:
It was not dark, it was not light,
Cold dews had drenched my plenteous hair
Through clay; you came to seek me there.
And Do you dream of me? you said.
My heart was dust that used to leap
To you; I answered half asleep:
My pillow is damp, my sheets are red,
There's a leaden tester to my bed;

Find you a warmer playfellow,
A warmer pillow for your head,
A kinder love to love than mine.
You wrung your hands, while I, like lead,
Crushed downwards through the sodden earth;
You smote your hands but not in mirth,
And reeled but were not drunk with wine.

For all night long I dreamed of you;
I woke and prayed against my will,
Then slept to dream of you again.
At length I rose and knelt and prayed.
I cannot write the words I said,
My words were slow, my tears were few;
But through the dark my silence spoke
Like thunder. When this morning broke,
My face was pinched, my hair was grey,
And frozen blood was on the sill
Where stifling in my struggle I lay.
If now you saw me you would say:
Where is the face I used to love?
And I would answer: Gone before;
It tarries veiled in paradise.
When once the morning star shall rise,
When earth with shadow flees away
And we stand safe within the door,
Then you shall lift the veil thereof.
Look up, rise up: for far above
Our palms are grown, our place is set;
There we shall meet as once we met,
And love with old familiar love.

THE THREAD OF LIFE
I
The irresponsive silence of the land,
The irresponsive sounding of the sea,
Speak both one message of one sense to me: -
Aloof, aloof, we stand aloof, so stand
Thou too aloof bound with the flawless band
Of inner solitude; we bind not thee;
But who from thy self-chain shall set thee free?
What heart shall touch thy heart? what hand thy hand? -
And I am sometimes proud and sometimes meek,
And sometimes I remember days of old
When fellowship seemed not so far to seek
And all the world and I seemed much less cold,
And at the rainbow's foot lay surely gold,
And hope felt strong and life itself not weak.

II

Thus am I mine own prison. Everything
Around me free and sunny and at ease:
Or if in shadow, in a shade of trees
Which the sun kisses, where the gay birds sing
And where all winds make various murmuring;
Where bees are found, with honey for the bees;
Where sounds are music, and where silences
Are music of an unlike fashioning.
Then gaze I at the merrymaking crew,
And smile a moment and a moment sigh
Thinking: Why can I not rejoice with you?
But soon I put the foolish fancy by:
I am not what I have nor what I do;
But what I was I am, I am even I.

III
Therefore myself is that one only thing
I hold to use or waste, to keep or give;
My sole possession every day I live,
And still mine own despite Time's winnowing.
Ever mine own, while moons and seasons bring
From crudeness ripeness mellow and sanitive;
Ever mine own, till Death shall ply his sieve;
And still mine own, when saints break grave and sing.
And this myself as king unto my King
I give, to Him Who gave Himself for me;
Who gives Himself to me, and bids me sing
A sweet new song of His redeemed set free;
he bids me sing: O death, where is thy sting?
And sing: O grave, where is thy victory?

BIRD RAPTURES
The sunrise wakes the lark to sing,
The moonrise wakes the nightingale.
Come darkness, moonrise, everything
That is so silent, sweet, and pale,
Come, so ye wake the nightingale.

Make haste to mount, thou wistful moon,
Make haste to wake the nightingale:
Let silence set the world in tune
To hearken to that wordless tale
Which warbles from the nightingale.

O herald skylark, stay thy flight
One moment, for a nightingale
Floods us with sorrow and delight.
To-morrow thou shalt hoist the sail,
Leave us tonight the nightingale.

TWILIGHT CALM
Oh, pleasant eventide!
Clouds on the western side
Grow grey and greyer, hiding the warm sun:
The bees and birds, their happy labours done,
Seek their close nests and bide.

Screened in the leafy wood
The stock-doves sit and brood:
The very squirrel leaps from bough to bough
But lazily; pauses; and settles now
Where once he stored his food.

One by one the flowers close,
Lily and dewy rose
Shutting their tender petals from the moon:
The grasshoppers are still; but not so soon
Are still the noisy crows.

The dormouse squats and eats
Choice little dainty bits
Beneath the spreading roots of a broad lime
Nibbling his fill he stops from time to time
And listens where he sits.

From far the lowings come
Of cattle driven home:
From farther still the wind brings fitfully
The vast continual murmur of the sea,
Now loud, now almost dumb.

The gnats whirl in the air,
The evening gnats; and there
The owl opes broad his eyes and wings to sail
For prey; the bat wakes; and the shell-less snail
Comes forth, clammy and bare.

Hark! that's the nightingale,
Telling the selfsame tale
Her song told when this ancient earth was young:
So echoes answered when her song was sung
In the first wooded vale.

We call it love and pain
The passion of her strain;
And yet we little understand or know:
Why should it not be rather joy that so
Throbs in each throbbing vein?

In separate herds the deer

Lie; here the bucks, and here
The does, and by its mother sleeps the fawn:
Through all the hours of night until the dawn
They sleep, forgetting fear.

The hare sleeps where it lies,
With wary half-closed eyes;
The cock has ceased to crow, the hen to cluck:
Only the fox is out, some heedless duck
Or chicken to surprise.

Remote, each single star
Comes out, till there they are
All shining brightly: how the dews fall damp!
While close at hand the glow-worm lights her lamp,
Or twinkles from afar.

But evening now is done
As much as if the sun
Day-giving had arisen in the East:
For night has come; and the great calm has ceased,
The quiet sands have run.

COBWEBS
It is a land with neither night nor day,
Nor heat nor cold, nor any wind, nor rain,
Nor hills nor valleys; but one even plain
Stretches thro' long unbroken miles away:
While through the sluggish air a twilight grey
Broodeth; no moons or seasons wax and wane,
No ebb and flow are there among the main,
No bud-time no leaf-falling there for aye,
No ripple on the sea, no shifting sand,
No beat of wings to stir the stagnant space,
And loveless sea: no trace of days before,
No guarded home, no time-worn resting place
No future hope, no fear forevermore.

www.ingramcontent.com/pod-product-compliance
Lightning Source LLC
Chambersburg PA
CBHW061311040426
42444CB00010B/2595